The White Cottage

I Talk You Talk Press

ISBN: 978-4-910971-23-0

www.italkyoutalk.com

info@italkyoutalk.com

CONTENTS

ACKNOWLEDGMENT

With thanks to Colin Dixon for sharing his story.
He is the original Old Jack.

INTRODUCTION

Hello my friends! I'm Old Jack. I live in the northwest of England, in a town near Liverpool. I'm retired now. I spend my time watching my hometown's rugby league club and writing ghost stories. I've written books of ghost stories from England, Scotland, Wales, Ireland, and Japan. I've also written a book about my memories of a rugby match, from when I was a young boy.

People often ask me why I'm interested in ghost stories. I just smile and tell them reading and writing about ghost stories is my hobby. But the story you are going to read now will give you the real answer. I hope you enjoy it.

1. THE INVITATION

Our story begins a few years after the end of the Second World War. I was fourteen, and lived with my mother and father in a small industrial town in the northwest of England. Our house was old and small, but it was warm and comfortable. My father worked in a local glass factory, but during the war, he was a soldier in the British Army. When he was in the army, he met another soldier called Owen Jones. Before the war, Owen lived in North Wales on his family's sheep farm. My father and Owen became best friends. When the war finished, they went back to their old lives, but they often wrote letters to each other.

One day in spring, a letter arrived from my father's old friend Owen Jones. When my mother and father read the letter, they were very excited. In the letter, there was an invitation. Owen invited our family to spend a few weeks during the summer holidays with him and his wife Beth on their sheep farm in North Wales. Their farm was called 'Hillcrest'. From the day the letter arrived to the day we left our town to go to Owen's farm, I was very excited. I was looking forward to our holiday. At school, I didn't listen to the teacher. I looked out of the window and thought about the holiday.

One sunny day in July, my family got on a train in Liverpool, and went to a town called Wrexham, which is on the border of Wales and England. As the train travelled south, I looked out of the window and watched the grey industrial towns of northwest England change to green fields and beautiful farmland. There were farm buildings and there seemed to be animals everywhere! There were sheep and cows in the fields. Then, I thought, *I am fourteen years of age, and this is the farthest I have ever been from my hometown. Because of the war and the dark years that followed, this is also the first time my family has been on holiday.*

I had never seen the countryside. All my life, I had only seen factories, old houses and grey landscapes. Looking out of the train window at the beautiful greenery, I felt like I was in another world.

2. ARRIVAL

When we arrived at Wrexham Station, Owen and Beth were waiting for us. They hugged me, my mother and my father. Owen smiled at me.

"So, you are Young Jack. Your father told me about you when we were in the army. It's good to meet you at last."

I smiled too. "It's good to meet you too," I said.

"You must be tired," said Beth. "Let's go to the farm so you can rest."

We got into Owen's big farm truck. I looked out of the window in silence at the beautiful Welsh countryside. The sun was shining and everything looked so green. I thought, *I will remember this summer for the rest of my life.*

I had no idea that I would remember the holiday for a different, stranger reason.

We arrived at Hillcrest farm in the mid-afternoon. Beth showed me my bedroom. It had a comfortable bed and antique furniture. From the window, I could see the green fields of the farm.

"I hope you like your room, Young Jack," said Beth.

"Oh, yes, I do. It's very nice," I said. "Thank you."

Owen and Beth ran the farm with the help of two local men from the nearby village, which was called Highcross. It was a large farm. It had sheep, cows, chickens and a few pigs. The noise they made filled the farmyard.

"Well," said Owen, "What do you think about the farm? Do you like it?"

My mother answered for us all. She said, "It's wonderful."

My mother and father said, "We will help with the farm work." So, the next day, we all helped to feed the animals and clean the farm buildings. I enjoyed it very much. Then, Owen said to me, "Young Jack, come to the sheep field. I'll show you how my sheep dog moves the sheep to a different field."

So Owen and I went to the large sheep field. He whistled, and his dog, Tess, moved the sheep from one field to another! I was so surprised!

"Tess is very clever," I said.

"Yes, she is," said Owen. "She helps us a lot on the farm."

Staying on the farm seemed like a dream to me. The sun was shining, the air was clean and fresh, and there was lots of food. At the end of the first week, Owen said,

"Well Young Jack, would you like to explore the local countryside by yourself and have an adventure?"

"Yes, I would," I said.

Owen went into a barn and came out with an old, but well-cared for bicycle.

"I've had this bicycle since I was a young boy. But it's still in good condition," he said. "Borrow it and travel around the area."

Owen, Beth and my parents decided that the next day, I would travel by bicycle to the village of Highcross. It was about two miles down the road from the farm. Owen said to my parents, "Don't worry. Young Jack won't get lost. There is only one road between the farm and village. He just has to follow that road. He will be safe."

3. THE WATERFALL

I set off on my adventure the next morning after breakfast. The sky was clear, and the air was fresh. The bicycle was good to ride. I cycled quickly along the road, which was empty except for a tractor. The tractor turned into a field and the driver waved to me. I waved back.

After about twenty minutes, I came to a sharp corner in the road. I slowed down and noticed a sign half-covered in tree branches. Next to the sign was a rough track which led into the forest that covered a hill. There was an arrow pointing down the track and the sign said 'Horse Head Falls'.

It's a waterfall, I thought. *I want to see it.*

I left the road and started to follow the track. The track was narrow, and it was difficult to ride the bicycle. I entered the dark forest. I was a little scared, but soon, I came out of the forest, and into an open space. In front of me was Horse Head Falls. I could see a very large stone near the top of the waterfall. It looked like a horse's head. Water poured down into the river below. I could feel the spray of water on my face. I never forgot that feeling. It was like a dream! I stayed at the waterfall for about twenty minutes, watching the water. I'd never seen anything like it before in my life. It was magical!

Then, I decided it was time to return to the road. I started to cycle down the track. It seemed harder than before, and I noticed other small tracks, which cut across the main track. After half an hour, I realised that I was lost!

I was sure that if I could get down the hill, I would find the edge of the forest. Then, in the open countryside, I would find the road to Highcross. So I cycled down the hill. I stayed on the wider tracks. There were fewer and fewer trees, and soon, at the bottom of the hill, the forest ended. I stopped. I was at the end of a long valley. On my left, there was a field with another rough track. I decided to follow that track.

4. THE COTTAGE

The track went around the trees, and went up a hill. On the right, there was a small stone cottage. The walls of the cottage were painted white. I cycled towards the cottage. Then, a man came out of a small building next to the cottage.

When he saw me, he waved at me. He looked around 60 years old. He was wearing rough work clothes. He walked towards me, smiling.

"Hello young man. Can I do anything for you?" he said.

I nodded. "I'm lost," I said. "I need directions to the road to Highcross."

Just then, a woman came out of the white cottage.

"James," she said. "Who are you talking to?"

"Just a young man asking for directions," said the man.

The woman came towards us.

"Well, ask him in for a drink," she said. "He looks very tired."

I put my bicycle against the wall of the small building and went into the cottage with them. They took me into the kitchen.

"Sit down," said the woman.

I sat at the large kitchen table while the woman made a pot of tea for us all.

"I've never seen you before," said the man.

"I'm staying at Hillcrest Farm," I said. "My parents and I are here on holiday for a few weeks. Today is my first trip away from the farm."

The couple introduced themselves as James and Maud Denby.

"This is our farm," said James. "It isn't as big as Hillcrest Farm, but it's enough for us."

As we drank our tea, I looked around the room. Everything seemed old and well-used. Above the fireplace there was an old clock. The time was 2:30. James saw me looking at the clock.

"That time isn't right," he said. "The clock stopped years ago. We planned to get it fixed, but we never did."

Next to the clock there was a photograph of a young man. He was wearing a naval uniform.

"That's our son, David," said James. "He joined the Navy when the war started."

James looked at his wife.

"We made a promise always to be here, waiting for him. Even if he was away for a long time."

Maud looked up from her teacup. "Around here, a promise made is a promise kept. David knows there will always be a home waiting for him here."

James looked at me. "Well, that's enough about us," he said. "So, young man, I'll give you directions back to the main road."

We all stood up and went outside. James said, "Continue on the track. It will turn to the left. Follow it up the hill, and you will see a gate. The road to Highcross runs straight past it. Turn right, and the village is about a quarter of a mile from there."

"Thank you for your help and kindness," I said.

James and Maud smiled.

"I hope someone would do the same for our son David if he was lost," said James.

I started to push my bicycle along the track. I turned around to wave goodbye, but James and Maud were already walking back into the house. I thought it was strange.

The war ended six years ago. Why isn't David at home? Maybe he ran away from the Navy during the war and is hiding somewhere, I thought.

5. THE VILLAGE

I cycled up the track, and came to a big gate. The road was next to the gate. On the gate, there was a sign in brightly painted letters – 'White Cottage Farm'.

I started to cycle on the road towards Highcross. Soon, I saw the village. I could see a church, post office, and a grocers and butchers. I stopped at a shop and bought a bottle of lemonade. I needed a rest, so I sat on one of the public benches next to a large stone cross in the centre of the village.

I had been sitting there for about ten minutes, when an old gentleman with a walking stick came and sat down on the bench. He looked at me and said, "Have you come from a place far away? I can see you're not from around here."

"I'm from northwest England," I said. "I'm staying at Hillcrest Farm for a few weeks."

"Ah, yes," said the man. "Owen and Beth's place. I know it well. Tell them Mr Williams said 'hello' when you see them."

"I will," I said. "I had an adventure today. I saw the waterfall, and then I got lost. But Mr and Mrs Denby from White Cottage Farm helped me."

Mr Williams looked at me. He looked a little angry. He leant forward towards me.

"Young man, you are very, very mistaken about your meeting with the Denbys. You didn't speak with them. I've lived here all my life, and I knew the Denbys very well. What you are saying isn't true."

I was confused and afraid. I had upset Mr Williams.

I asked, "But why are you so sure?"

Mr Williams sighed and leant back on the bench.

"One night in May 1941 during the war, there was a large German bombing raid in Liverpool, northeast of here. Anti-aircraft guns around the city fought a brave battle against the German bombers. Some of the German pilots became afraid and decided to return home to Germany. But first, they dropped their bombs. They were flying in darkness over the North Wales countryside. They couldn't see anything below. They dropped their bombs into the valley near the village. This made the planes lighter, so they could get back to Germany more quickly. White Cottage Farm was hit by a bomb, and James and Maud were both killed."

I looked at Mr Williams. I was shocked.

"I will never forget that night," said Mr Williams. The bombs hit the valley at two thirty in the morning. Everything was in chaos. Some of us went up to the Denbys' farm, and found it had been destroyed."

Mr Williams' eyes looked sad.

"So, you see young man. You are very mistaken."

He stood up, and without saying anything else, he walked away.

6. THE RETURN

I was so confused. Was I wrong? Mr Williams seemed to be telling the truth.

What should I do? I thought. *I'll go back to the farm and tell James and Maud about Mr Williams' story.*

I rode up the road towards the cottage. Soon, I was at the gate.

"What?" I said. "I don't understand."

The gate was damaged. There was no painted sign. Weeds and grass were growing around the gate. I got off my bicycle and walked down the track.

The cottage will be here, just around the corner, I thought.

I walked past some trees and around the corner. I stopped. There was no cottage. There was only large stones and broken wood on the ground. I started to panic. The building where I had left my bicycle was gone. There were just more stones in its place. I walked past it and went towards the cottage. I stood in the space of the room where I had drunk tea with James and Maud. I remembered the taste of the tea in my mouth.

I was shocked. The cottage was gone. There were no walls. There was no door. And James and Maud were not there.

This is so strange, I thought. *It's unbelievable! I don't understand this at all.*

I started to feel scared. I ran back to my bicycle next to the damaged gate. When I was riding back to Hillcrest Farm, I couldn't stop thinking about the cottage.

Should I tell my parents and Owen and Beth? I thought. *No, no one will believe me. My parents will think I am ill. Maybe Owen and Beth knew James and Maud. Maybe they will react like Mr Williams. I don't want to upset them.*

I arrived back at Hillcrest Farm. My parents and Owen and Beth were in the living room.

"How was your day, Young Jack?" asked Owen.

"It was wonderful," I said. "The countryside was beautiful. I saw a waterfall. Then, I went into the village."

"It's very different from your hometown, isn't it?" said Beth, smiling. "I'm glad you had a good time."

Two weeks later, my parents and I left Hillcrest Farm and North Wales. On the train going back home, I thought about James and Maud and the cottage. It was strange.

When we returned to our town, we went back to our daily routines. I went back to school and my father went to work. The holiday in North Wales seemed like a dream.

7. LATER YEARS

As time passed, I started to understand more. The clock in the cottage said '2:30'. It was broken. Mr Williams had said, "The bombs hit the valley at two thirty in the morning".

Was that a coincidence? Or was it a sign that someone, or something, in the ghost world wanted that time to be remembered? Maud had said, "David knows there will always be a home waiting for him here". They were waiting for their son. They promised him they would wait for him to return after the war.

Later I did some research and found out that David was killed in the war a few days after his parents were killed. Are their ghosts still waiting for him?

Did I see ghosts? Or did I see a memory in the stones where the cottage used to be?

I never forgot that day in North Wales. I never told anyone about my experience, but I often thought about James and Maud. I knew what I had seen and heard that day. That is why I became interested in ghosts.

When I was older, I started to research ghost stories. When I retired, it became my hobby. I wrote some books about ghost stories from England, Scotland, Ireland, Wales and Japan.

I returned to North Wales many times over the years. But I never returned to White Cottage Farm.

I am old now, but I still ask myself, "Is the clock still stopped at 2:30? Are James and Maud still waiting for their son to come home?" Maud said, 'Around here, a promise made is a promise kept. David knows there will always be a home waiting for him here'.

They promised their son that they would be there. David can't come home, but James and Maud should be left to rest in peace.

THANK YOU

Thank you for reading The White Cottage. (Word count: 3,153) Old Jack hopes you enjoyed his story.

Old Jack has written a series of ghost story books.
Old Jack's Ghost Stories from England (1)
Old Jack's Ghost Stories from England (2)
Old Jack's Ghost Stories from Scotland
Old Jack's Ghost Stories from Wales
Old Jack's Ghost Stories from Ireland
Old Jack's Ghost Stories from Japan

He has also written a memoir from when he was a young boy, about a rugby match he watched with his father.
Match Day

If you would like to read more graded readers, please visit our website http://www.italkyoutalk.com

Other Level 3 graded readers include
A Dangerous Weekend
A Holiday to Remember
Akiko and Amy Part 1
Akiko and Amy Part 2
Akiko and Amy Part 3
Be My Valentine

Children of Another Planet
Different Seas
Enjoy Your Business Trip
Enjoy Your Homestay
I'm Late!
I Need a Friend
Let's Do It!
Lincoln Takes a Trip
Match Day
Old Jack's Ghost Stories from England (1)
Old Jack's Ghost Stories from England (2)
Old Jack's Ghost Stories from Ireland
Old Jack's Ghost Stories from Japan
Old Jack's Ghost Stories from Scotland
Old Jack's Ghost Stories from Wales
Party Time!
Pretty and Bright
Roger's Long Ride
Rona
Stories for Christmas
Summer Days
The Curse
The Diary
Time to Go
Together Again
Travellers' Tales
Wall of Secrets
Who is Holly?
Wintertime

ABOUT THE AUTHOR

I Talk You Talk Press is an award-winning Japan-based publisher of language textbooks, graded readers and language learning/teaching resources. We won the Language Learner Literature Award in 2019 and 2020.

Our team is made up of highly experienced language teachers and translators, who have all studied at least one additional language to an advanced level.

This experience enables us to design our materials from the perspective of both the teacher and the learner. We consult with both teachers and language learners when designing our textbooks and graded readers, and test our materials extensively in the classroom before publication.

We are a fast-growing press, and currently publish graded readers for learners of English. We publish new graded readers monthly.

www.ingramcontent.com/pod-product-compliance
Lightning Source LLC
LaVergne TN
LVHW042241190726
843491LV00003BA/1172

9784910971230